WART
CORRESPONDENCE

BETWEEN

PRESIDENT ROOSEVELT

AND

POPE PIUS XII

With an Introduction & Explanatory Notes
by MYRON C. TAYLOR
Personal Representative of the President
of the United States of America
to His Holiness Pope Pius XII

THE MACMILLAN COMPANY · *New York*
1947

PRINTED IN THE UNITED STATES OF AMERICA

Designed by Oscar Ogg

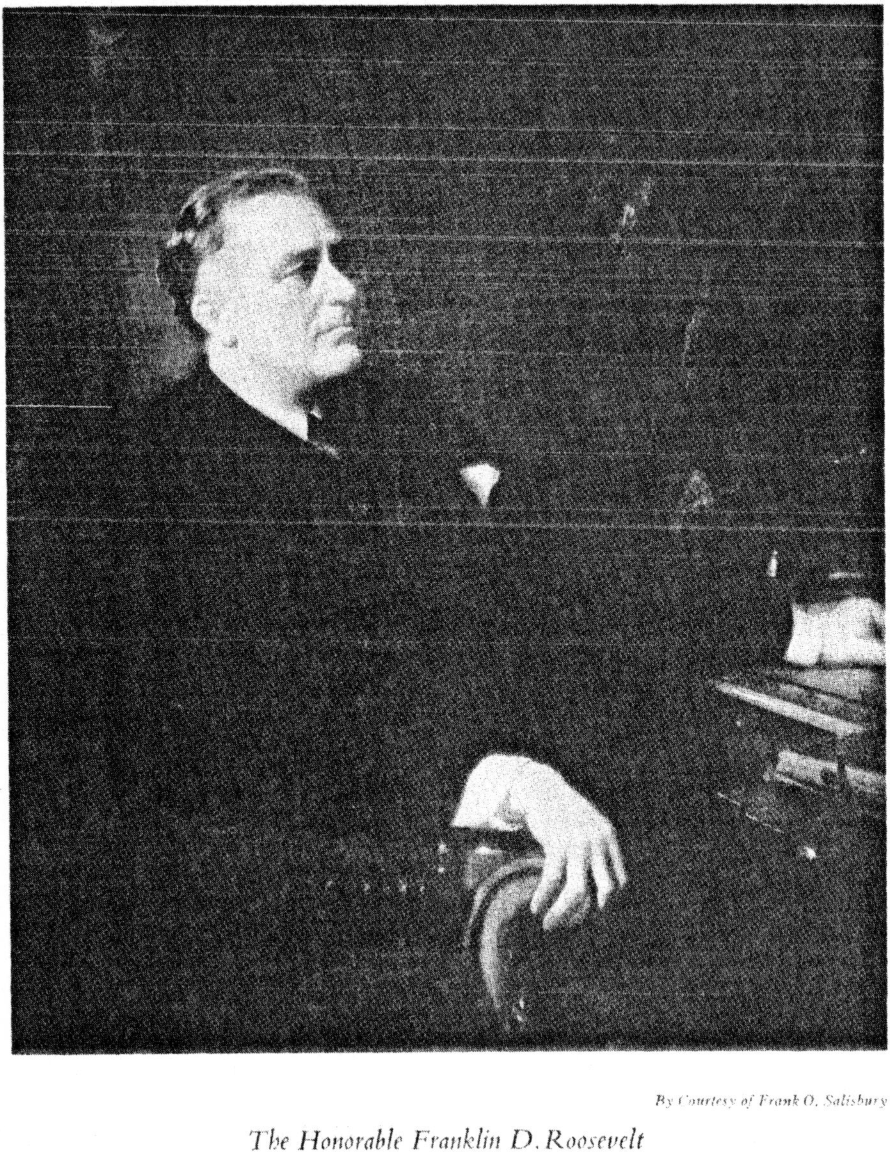

By Courtesy of Frank O. Salisbury

The Honorable Franklin D. Roosevelt

By Courtesy of Fabbrica di San Pietro

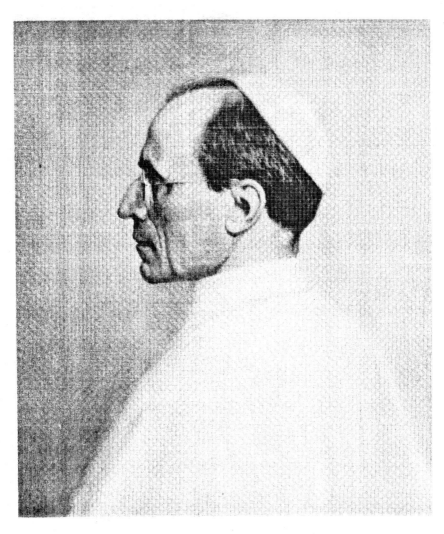

His Holiness Pope Pius XII

CONTENTS

ix

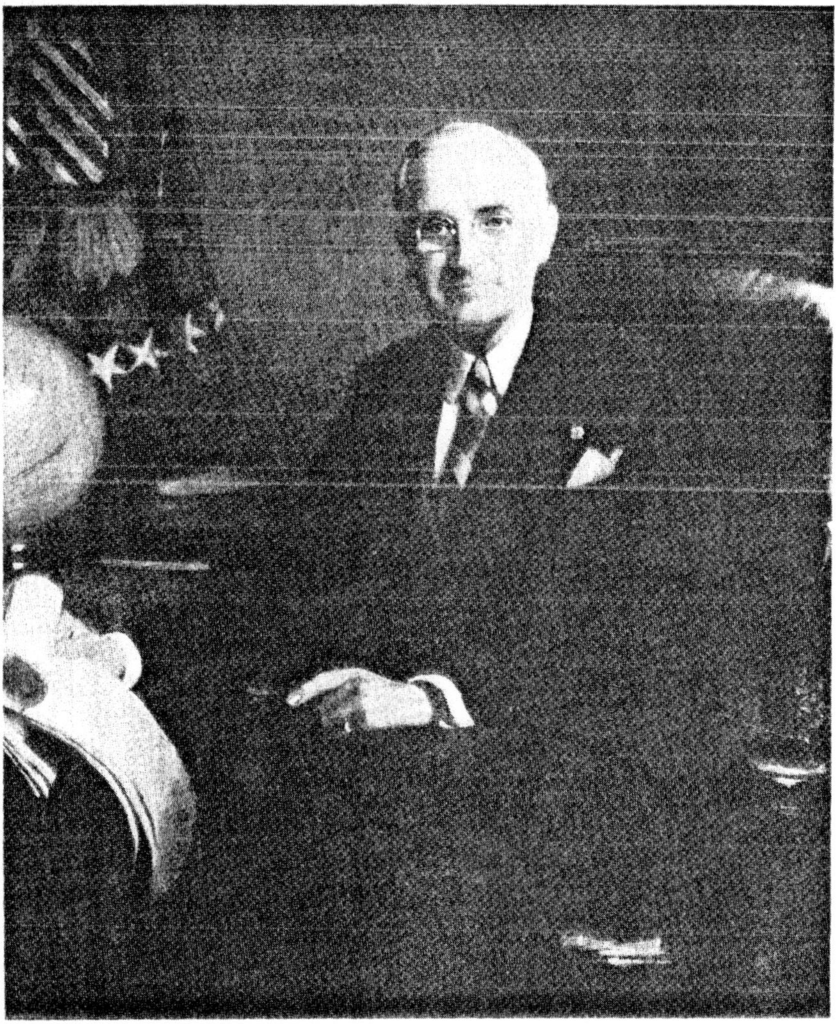

By Courtesy of Frank O. Salisbury

The Honorable Harry S. Truman, President of the United States of America

PREFACE

BY

THE HONORABLE HARRY S. TRUMAN

President of the United States

It is in the American tradition of open diplomacy that the world should be given the texts of the messages exchanged between my lamented predecessor and His Holiness the Pope. This correspondence began in the dark days of December 1939, when President Roosevelt, animated by the desire to work for peace and the alleviation of human suffering more effectively through parallel efforts by those in government and those in religion, sent Honorable Myron C. Taylor on a Special Mission as his Personal Representative to His Holiness.

Mr. Taylor arrived in Italy for his first visit in the dangerous and uncertain days of 1940, days which were the forerunner of even more tragic sorrows to come as the war widened and suffering overspread the world. Thereafter he has gone to Rome from time to time as circumstances warranted.

The objectives and accomplishments of these great endeavors, alike in the field of humanitarian activity and in seeking an enduring peace, are reflected in the messages exchanged between the late President and His Holiness, the texts of which are now given publication.

These messages, written during a momentous period of history, constitute a record of incalculable value. That record belongs to all who sought through victory, and continue to seek, the blessings of universal peace and security and well-being. It will be read with interest and appreciation by our contemporaries and will have a permanent place in the history of the greatest war in the annals of mankind.

THE WHITE HOUSE, *October 1, 1946*   HARRY S. TRUMAN

PREFACE
BY

HIS HOLINESS POPE PIUS XII

The late Honorable Franklin D. Roosevelt, President of the United States, in his letter addressed to Us on the 14th of February 1940 clearly set forth the purpose he had in mind in sending his Personal Representative to the Holy See. It was that the one so designated by him would be "the channel of communication for any views You and I might wish to exchange in the interest of concord among the peoples of the world."

The correspondence published herewith and the observations and references to be found therein, brief though they be at times and occasioned by circumstances, show how well the appointment has served the purpose intended. Its full significance however was much more far-reaching than this, as may be gathered from a perusal of the letters themselves.

The fortunate outcome of numberless occurrences which arose both during the course of the war and in the post-war period, the solution of urgent problems, the interchange of important information, the organization of American relief which flowed in such generous streams to alleviate the misery begotten of the war, all these would have been well nigh unthinkable and almost impossible, were it not for the designation of a Personal Representative of the President and the magnanimous cooperation and achievements of His Excellency, Mr. Myron Taylor.

PIUS PP. XII

FROM THE VATICAN, *August 6, 1946*

Introduction by
Myron C. Taylor

INTRODUCTION
BY
MYRON C. TAYLOR

The publication on the second anniversary of President Roosevelt's death of the wartime correspondence between him and Pope Pius XII is undertaken, with the authority and approval of President Truman and of His Holiness, as a tribute to one extremely important manifestation of the forward-looking leadership of the great War President. Messages were exchanged over the period from December, 1939, when President Roosevelt decided to send a Personal Representative to His Holiness, until the end of 1944. The last messages in this volume are the Pope's poignant condolences sent to President Truman and to Mrs. Roosevelt on April 13, 1945, the day after the sudden and untimely ending of Franklin Delano Roosevelt's life shocked the entire civilized world.

*

In all his efforts for world peace and the betterment of mankind, President Roosevelt was always conscious of the fundamental strength in human affairs of moral and spiritual forces. Throughout the early years of his Presidency, aided by the far-seeing statesmanship of Secretary of State Cordell Hull, Mr. Roosevelt placed every resource of his gifted talents, his unusual personality, and his high office in the service of the preservation of peace, of amity and understanding among nations, and of the material and spiritual advancement of the individual human being. The vision—the hope—of Franklin D. Roosevelt was a world order built upon firm moral and political foundations, upon the principle of the Good Neighbor, upon economic progress and social justice, upon the essential human freedoms, and upon respect for the dignity of the human soul. Toward the attainment of that hope he exercised his highest powers of constructive leadership. As the moral and political bulwarks of world peace collapsed one by one in the swiftly deteriorating circumstances of the late thirties, he sought to stay the hands raised against peace and to clarify for the peoples of his own and of other lands the true character of the perils which threatened them.

The outbreak of war in Europe put a ruthless ending to all efforts for the preservation of peace. It became necessary for our own country to place itself in a position of adequate self-defense in the face of increasing uncertainties and of emerging dangers to our own peaceful existence. It also became imperative for us in our own best national interest to exercise our influence and leadership to prevent, if possible, the spread of war; to explore all possibilities of bringing the war to a quick and just conclusion; to assuage the human suffering caused by the hostilities; and to lay the foundations for a better world after the termination of the conflict. It was to these great tasks of self-defense, of humanity, and of peace that President Roosevelt turned his attention after Hitler's mechanized forces hurled themselves upon Poland on September 1, 1939.

The President was convinced that a closer association in all parts of the free world between those in government and those in religion who shared common ideals was essential to the end that their thought and action could be brought unitedly to bear upon the vast problems of peace and of the suffering that loomed ahead. Accordingly, on December 23, 1939, in messages to leaders of the Catholic, Protestant, and Jewish faiths, he proposed that political and religious forces undertake to re-enforce, by direct discussions, their respective endeavors for peace and the alleviation of human suffering.

In these letters, addressed to His Holiness Pope Pius XII, to the President of the Federal Council of the Churches of Christ

2

in America, Dr. George A. Buttrick, and to the President of the Jewish Theological Seminary of America, Rabbi Cyrus Adler, the President expressed his deep hope "that all of the churches of the world which believe in a common God will throw the great weight of their influence into this great cause." Looking to parallel action for the re-establishment of peace when the day for that came, and for the alleviation of suffering during the war, he invited the leaders of the Protestant and Jewish faiths resident in the United States to come to Washington from time to time to discuss problems with him personally. To His Holiness in Rome, with whom personal exchanges of views were possible only through correspondence and a trusted intermediary, he suggested sending a Personal Representative to act as a channel of communication and an instrument of similar discussions.

These letters met with immediate and cordial acceptance by the leaders of the three faiths, and the ensuing years witnessed a mobilization of the moral and spiritual forces of mankind on a scale of widespread influence never before seen in history. This glorious effort will ever be a monument to the memory of President Roosevelt.

*

It was my great privilege and honor to have been chosen as the President's Personal Representative to the Pope. When the President telephoned on the evening of December 22, 1939, to ask me to undertake this task of high trust and responsibility, I was serving as his Personal Representative on the Intergovernmental Committee on Political Refugees, to the work of which he had called me in April of the preceding year shortly after my retirement from business activities. On a number of occasions during my service on the Intergovernmental Committee, I had been in touch with the Vatican which was likewise active in carrying forward that great humanitarian work. It

3

appeared to the President that the new responsibility which he desired to entrust to me if agreeable also to the Pope, would be both a continuation and an extension of the vital field of endeavor in which I was already engaged.

On the morning of December 23 I undertook to carry out the new mission to the best of my ability, and to leave for Rome as soon as health permitted. The agreeability of this choice to His Holiness was conveyed to the President by the Apostolic Delegate in Washington, Archbishop Amleto Giovanni Cicognani, through the services of Archbishop Francis J. Spellman. His Holiness wrote personally to the President on January 7, 1940, responding with appreciation to all of the President's suggestions.

Happily for the friendly association thus begun, His Holiness was not a stranger to the President, or to me. In the autumn of 1936, Cardinal Eugenio Pacelli, who three years later was elected Pope and who was then Secretary of State under Pope Pius XI, had visited the United States and had talked with the President at Hyde Park. The basis of their mutual respect was laid and their mutual appreciation of each other's qualities of leadership was begun in those talks. During the same trip Cardinal Pacelli had been a guest in my home in New York. The President had visited Italy, and I had frequently spent brief periods of time there, particularly in Florence, where I had maintained a home for many years. Most fortunate conditions for readily undertaking personal discussions accordingly existed at the very beginning of the exchange of views between the President and the Pope. While both the President and I were of Episcopalian faith, we, with America as a whole, regarded the cause of peace and the amelioration of human distress during the war as in no sense either sectarian or partisan, but instead as universal to all men seeking the well-being of mankind in a peaceful world under moral law.

The activities initiated at the end of 1939 began at a time

when, under dire threat to their peace and even survival, nations in or near the theater of war in Europe faced the future without a shred of dependable security against attack. Some responded with passive hope, some with determination, all with weakness compared with the ready forces of the enemy. Nations farther away were not only affected in nearly every aspect of daily individual and national life, but were confronted with the grave possibilities of witnessing aggression once again crowned with victory and even of attack eventually upon themselves. Our own country's hope of living at peace in a world of friendly neighbors was gravely in jeopardy.

The President had made every practicable effort to prevent the onset of the war. His Holiness had done likewise in the sphere of the Church. Both now sought to prevent the war from spreading, as well as to commence the consideration of the bases of an enduring peace in the future, which would lift the burdens of warring and distress from the backs of all men. Efforts toward the first objective had long been under way in the Department of State, and Secretary of State Cordell Hull had just organized an Advisory Committee on Problems of Foreign Relations, composed of his associates in the Department, to assist him in considering problems of peace.

The President asked me, just before my departure for Rome on February 16, to undertake discussions especially on four bases of peace which he had been turning over in his mind. These were freedom of religion, freedom of communication of news and knowledge, reduction of armament, and freedom of trade between nations. It was also desired that estimates and impressions concerning a possible early ending of the war should be explored in all quarters with which I would come in touch. I carried with me for His Holiness a letter of credence, dated February 14, in which the President laid stress upon his hope that through parallel endeavors "the common ideals of religion and of humanity itself can have united expression for the re-establishment of a more permanent peace . . ." His Holiness received me on February 27, and asked me to convey His warmest personal regards to President Roosevelt. Thus began the first of seven visits. Two were as brief as one or two weeks. Four were as long as a month or longer. One was a year in duration.

*

It was necessary promptly to organize a small office for the conduct of work. Although—as earlier in connection with the special work for refugees—the President had conferred on me the honorary rank of Ambassador in order to facilitate adequately the official representation abroad of our Chief Executive, he desired to distinguish all aspects of my office from those of a diplomatic embassy. He equally desired to make clear that the Personal Representative's mission was to His Holiness personally rather than to the Vatican as such. The office, therefore, was established in my own apartment in Rome, and continued there excepting during the emergency period while Italy was at war with the United States, which temporarily required its location in Vatican City.

The staff consisted of an assistant, Mr. Harold H. Tittmann, detached for special duty from the American Foreign Service, and, in due course, a personal secretary and a clerk. Subsequently, during the crowded year between the liberation of Rome and the establishment again of a fully functioning American diplomatic mission to the Government of Italy, when for a time my office was the only civilian American agency in Italy, the staff was augmented by a second assistant, Mr. Franklin C. Gowen, who afterward remained as sole assistant, and temporarily also by three additional clerks.

The work of the office with respect both to the American Embassy in Rome and to the Department of State in Washington was so organized as to provide, apart from such matters as the President or His Holiness regarded as of reserved confi-

6

dence, for the fullest exchange of information and other co-operation concerning its work. The reports submitted to President Roosevelt were customarily transmitted by him to the Secretary of State. Usually, while in Rome or while travelling to and from Rome, opportunity was taken at the same time, on the President's request, for personal discussions with foreign officials on the currents of thought in their countries and in ours, and with American officials especially on developments at home.

While naturally the main subjects of discussion contemplated within the purposes of the mission were considered directly between His Holiness and the Personal Representative of the President, other matters, particularly detailed relief problems and arrangements for presentation of visiting Americans requesting to be received by His Holiness, were largely raised with the officials of the Secretariat of State of His Holiness. Among these officials were the able and always helpful Secretary of State, Cardinal Luigi Maglione (until his regrettable decease soon after the liberation of Rome), and the two principal Under Secretaries of State, Monsignor Domenico Tardini and Monsignor Giovanni B. Montini, on both of whom it was always possible to depend for sympathetic and intelligent consideration of problems, whether burdensome or not. In the periods between my visits to Rome, matters needing attention were referred to my assistant there or were considered by me in the United States by telegraph or through the distinguished Apostolic Delegate in Washington, Archbishop Cicognani.

In the first audience, His Holiness extended to me a gracious invitation to call without formal appointment in order that our conversations could occur whenever mutual convenience served and as often as circumstances warranted. In view of the vast and complex problems raised in considering the bases of world peace, and the manifold problems which the attempts to relieve the war's human suffering entailed, discussions between us were held frequently throughout the periods of my various visits to

Rome. To this may be attributed in some degree that accumulation of mutual understanding and clarification of common views which gradually resulted and which equally gratified President Roosevelt and His Holiness.

I wish in these pages to express my lasting gratitude to my associates for their superb devotion to duty, oftentimes in conditions of personal danger, and to my wife, Anabel Taylor, whose courageous and ever-thoughtful assistance and support eased for me many of the difficulties which I gladly faced in the discharge of my responsibilities.

*

President Roosevelt and Pope Pius XII carried on their parallel endeavors for more than five years, which all but covered the entire span of the most deadly attack on the foundations of Christian civilization and the most exhausting strife in mankind's annals. Upon the outcome of that war the future course of mankind had been staked. Its issues were ultimate and uncompromising, and their true character had been discerned almost too late. Victory had come perilously close to being lost throughout the first half of these years. It was finally won only by the aroused and united strength and will of every force in the world, armed and unarmed, determined to survive and build at last for mankind a peace with security, justice, and moral and material well-being—a peace to be guarded vigilantly, and enforced when need be.

For "this great cause" President Roosevelt had striven with all his life's strength. The co-work between him and Pope Pius XII and others in the spiritual and humanitarian spheres of like devotion to this cause at home and abroad, was a manifestation of his inspired efforts to give to the world's moral forces, during these years of fateful crisis, unity of goal and plan, leadership in concerting their influence, encouragement for their humanitarian services to alleviate suffering, and common expression of their hopes and purposes in the future decisions as to the peace and welfare of mankind. While their leadership was from a national position on one hand and a religious position on the other, the challenge they confronted and accepted was, at bottom, a moral one, and their respective efforts were for moral objectives.

The respect and friendship between tne President and His Holiness allowed them freely to exchange views and to labor, with failures and successes, for the accomplishment of their common purposes. Despite the most constructive efforts each could make, their independent efforts, made without prior consultation but for the same ends, to prevent the outbreak of the world war had been defeated by circumstances not alter- able except by prepared military power. After the war had begun, their efforts to prevent its spread, particularly as regards Italy, had likewise failed. But their further labors were fruitful of constructive results: the lifting of the weight of suffering in all places that the hands of sympathy and help could reach to bring succor and comfort; the avoidance of misunderstanding of the spirit and inıentions of the United Nations in the fighting in Italy; the ending of the war without confusion among the many moral forces which had found expression in these en- deavors; the hope and encouragement to strive for a better life for men and nations in the future, which helped to provide firm purpose and steadiness of courage in an era of upheaval and profound questioning; and the widening of areas of com- mon views concerning the bases on which to build just and enduring peace.

The world was fortunate indeed to have had in its darkest hour the vitality of leadership of which the parallel endeavors were a part—a leadership which placed these vital activities upon so high a moral, spiritual and humanitarian plane.

The opportunity of representing President Roosevelt in his exchanges of views with Pope Pius XII in the service of the great cause to which they were both dedicated is the source for me of most cherished reflection. It was my good fortune to have been chosen to be the means for conveying from one to the other the innermost thoughts of two men of such eminence of world stature and of such talent and devotion as President Franklin D. Roosevelt and His Holiness Pope Pius XII. It is my hope that the inspiration that one could not fail to receive from long and intimate talks with President Roosevelt and His Holiness on mankind's great problems may in some measure be shared by all men through the reading and study of the messages which they exchanged.

These messages are the essential record of the fruitful discussions and efforts carried on by two great leaders. They do not of themselves, of course, reflect all the circumstances of the time or present fully all the specific problems to which they refer. While not assuming the privilege of supplementing them, I have nevertheless taken the liberty of making a few explanatory notes in order to place these notable messages within the framework of the continuing relationship in which they were written. The messages, period by period, comprise ten groups of exchanges of views, and are so arranged here.

*

The efforts in course when the untimely death of President Roosevelt intervened were continued without interruption by President Harry S. Truman. At that time, in 1945, the ardent hopes of mankind for friendly understanding and real neighborliness, for the binding up of the wounds of war, for reconstruction of conditions of material and moral well-being, and for the establishment of true peace and security in the world, were yet to be realized. The path was obscured by the shadows of past events, the perplexities of the present, and the uncertainties of the future. Faith alone could look to the horizon of the better day all mankind yearned to see. The war had consequences too far-reaching and penetrating in all aspects of social, economic and political life for these hopes to be attained quickly.

Profound conflicts of principle and policy continued to persist in many quarters of the globe.

In the spring of 1946, President Truman requested me to visit Rome again for further exchanges of views with His Holiness. On that occasion, he gave expression both to the world's need and to his own convictions that every resource must be employed to bring enduring peace to the troubled peoples of the world. He said:

"There is no minimizing the gravity of the days in which we live. I feel the necessity of having for my guidance the counsel and cooperation of all men and women of good will whether in religion, in government, or in the pursuits of everyday life. I have therefore sought the advice of leaders in religion of various convictions and allegiances not only in this country but from abroad. I feel that all have a vital contribution to make. I shall continue to welcome the counsel of such leaders to the end that the voice of conscience may be heard in the councils of nations as they seek a solution of that age-old problem: the government of man."

It was with these noble thoughts to guide me that I proceeded to Rome last summer and again in the late autumn for brief visits.

No better opportunity will perhaps ever come to express my deep sense of the honor extended me by the confidence of President Roosevelt and President Truman and by the trust and friendliness of His Holiness the Pope. It is my prayerful hope that, with God's help, our President and Pope Pius XII and all men of good will may continue to seek and to accomplish, within the limit of human capacity, the realization of the great ideals for the vindication of which mankind so heroically endured its greatest trial of war.

WASHINGTON, D. C., *January 18, 1947*

The First Exchange
of
Messages

EXPLANATORY NOTE

The two messages which follow represent the first exchange in the correspondence between President Roosevelt and Pope Pius XII. Reference has already been made in the Introduction to the circumstances under which this correspondence was initiated.

*These messages set forth at length the thoughts which actuated the two men in embarking upon their parallel endeavors for peace and the alleviation of human suffering through a mobilization of the moral forces of mankind.—*M. C. T.

I

Letter from President Roosevelt to His Holiness

DECEMBER 23, 1939

Your Holiness:

Because, at this Christmas time, the world is in sorrow, it is especially fitting that I send you a message of greeting and of faith.

The world has created for itself a civilization capable of
giving to mankind security and peace firmly set in the foundations of religious teachings. Yet, though it has conquered the
earth, the sea, and even the air, civilization today passes through
war and travail.

I take heart in remembering that in a similar time, Isaiah
first prophesied the birth of Christ. Then, several centuries
before His coming, the condition of the world was not unlike
that which we see today. Then, as now, a conflagration had
been set; and nations walked dangerously in the light of the
fires they had themselves kindled. But in that very moment a
spiritual rebirth was foreseen,—a new day which was to loose
the captives and to consume the conquerors in the fire of their
own kindling; and those who had taken the sword were to
perish by the sword. There was promised a new age wherein
through renewed faith the upward progress of the human race
would become more secure.

Again, during the several centuries which we refer to as the
Dark Ages, the flame and sword of barbarians swept over
Western civilization; and, again, through a re-kindling of the
inherent spiritual spark in mankind, another rebirth brought
back order and culture and religion.

I believe that the travail of today is a new form of these old
conflicts. Because the tempo of all worldly things has been so

greatly accelerated in these modern days we can hope that the period of darkness and destruction will be vastly shorter than in the olden times.

In their hearts men decline to accept, for long, the law of destruction forced upon them by wielders of brute force. Always they seek, sometimes in silence, to find again the faith without which the welfare of nations and the peace of the world cannot be rebuilt.

I have the rare privilege of reading the letters and confidences of thousands of humble people, living in scores of different nations. Their names are not known to history, but their daily work and courage carry on the life of the world. I know that these, and uncounted numbers like them in every country, are looking for a guiding light. We remember that the Christmas Star was first seen by shepherds in the hills, long before the leaders knew of the Great Light which had entered the world.

I believe that while statesmen are considering a new order of things, the new order may well be at hand. I believe that it is even now being built, silently but inevitably, in the hearts of masses whose voices are not heard, but whose common faith will write the final history of our time. They know that unless there is belief in some guiding principle and some trust in a divine plan, nations are without light, and peoples perish. They know that the civilization handed down to us by our fathers was built by men and women who knew in their hearts that all were brothers because they were children of God. They believe that by His will enmities can be healed; that in His mercy the weak can find deliverance, and the strong can find grace in helping the weak.

In the grief and terror of the hour, these quiet voices, if they can be heard, may yet tell of the re-building of the world.

It is well that the world should think of this at Christmas.

Because the people of this nation have come to a realization that time and distance no longer exist in the older sense, they understand that that which harms one segment of humanity harms all the rest. They know that only by friendly association between the seekers of light and the seekers of peace everywhere can the forces of evil be overcome.

In these present moments, no spiritual leader, no civil leader can move forward on a specific plan to terminate destruction and build anew. Yet the time for that will surely come.

It is, therefore, my thought that though no given action or given time may now be prophesied, it is well that we encourage a closer association between those in every part of the world—those in religion and those in government—who have a common purpose.

I am, therefore, suggesting to Your Holiness that it would give me great satisfaction to send to You my personal representative in order that our parallel endeavors for peace and the alleviation of suffering may be assisted.

When the time shall come for the re-establishment of world peace on a surer foundation, it is of the utmost importance to humanity and to religion that common ideals shall have united expression.

Furthermore, when that happy day shall dawn, great problems of practical import will face us all. Millions of people of all races, all nationalities and all religions may seek new lives by migration to other lands or by re-establishment of old homes. Here, too, common ideals call for parallel action.

I trust, therefore, that all of the churches of the world which believe in a common God will throw the great weight of their influence into this great cause.

To You, whom I have the privilege of calling a good friend and an old friend, I send my respectful greetings at this Christmas Season.

Cordially yours,

FRANKLIN DELANO ROOSEVELT

19

II

Reply of His Holiness to President Roosevelt

JANUARY 7, 1940

Your Excellency:

The memorable message that Your Excellency was pleased to have forwarded to Us on the eve of the Holy Feast of Christ-mas has brightened with a ray of consolation, of hope and confidence, the suffering, the heart-rending fear and the bitter-ness of the peoples caught up in the vortex of war. For this all right-minded men have paid you the spontaneous tribute of their sincere gratitude.

We have been deeply moved by the noble thought con-tained in your note, in which the spirit of Christmas and the desire to see it applied to the great human problems have found such eloquent expression; and fully persuaded of its extra-ordinary importance We lost no time in communicating it to the distinguished gathering present that very morning in the Consistorial Hall of this Apostolic Vatican Palace, solemnly expressing before the world, Catholic and non-Catholic alike, Our appreciation of this courageous document, inspired by a far-seeing statesmanship and a profound human sympathy.

We have been particularly impressed by one characteristic feature of Your Excellency's message; the vital, spiritual contact with the thoughts and the feelings, the hopes and the aspirations of the masses of the people, of those classes, namely, on whom more than others, and in a measure never felt before, weighs the burden of sorrow and sacrifice imposed by the present restless and tempestuous hour. Also for this reason none perhaps better than We can understand the meaning, the revealing power and the warmth of feeling manifest in this act of Your Excellency.

In fact Our own daily experience tells Us of the deep-seated yearning for peace that fills the hearts of the common people. In the measure that the war with its direct and indirect repercussions spreads; and the more economic, social and family life is forcibly wrenched from its normal bases by the continuation of the war, and is forced along the way of sacrifice and every kind of privation, the bitter need of which is not always plain to all; so much the more intense is the longing for peace that pervades the hearts of men and their determination to find and to apply the means that lead to peace.

When that day dawns—and We would like to hope that it is not too far distant—on which the roar of battle will lapse into silence and there will arise the possibility of establishing a true and sound peace dictated by the principles of justice and equity, only he will be able to discern the path that should be followed who unites with high political power a clear understanding of the voice of humanity along with a sincere reverence for the divine precepts of life as found in the Gospel of Christ. Only men of such moral stature will be able to create the peace, that will compensate for the incalculable sacrifices of this war and clear the way for a comity of nations, fair to all, efficacious and sustained by mutual confidence.

We are fully aware of how stubborn the obstacles are that stand in the way of attaining this goal, and how they become daily more difficult to surmount. And if the friends of peace do not wish their labors to be in vain, they should visualize distinctly the seriousness of these obstacles, and the consequently slight probability of immediate success so long as the present state of the opposing forces remains essentially unchanged.

As Vicar on earth of the Prince of Peace, from the first days of Our Pontificate We have dedicated Our efforts and Our solicitude to the purpose of maintaining peace, and afterwards of re-establishing it. Heedless of momentary lack of success and of the difficulties involved, We are continuing to follow along the path marked out for Us by Our Apostolic mission. As We walk this path, often rough and thorny, the echo which reaches Us from countless souls, both within and outside the Church together with the consciousness of duty done, is for Us abundant and consoling reward.

And now that in this hour of world-wide pain and mis-giving the Chief Magistrate of the great Northern American Federation, under the spell of the Holy Night of Christmas, should have taken such a prominent place in the vanguard of those who would promote peace and generously succor the victims of the war, bespeaks a providential help, which We acknowledge with grateful joy and increased confidence. It is an exemplary act of fraternal and hearty solidarity between the New and the Old World in defence against the chilling breath of aggressive and deadly godless and antichristian tendencies, that threaten to dry up the fountainhead whence civilization has come and drawn its strength.

In such circumstances We shall find a special satisfaction, as We have already informed Your Excellency, in receiving with all the honor due to his well-known qualifications and to the dignity of his important mission, the representative who is to be sent to Us as the faithful interpreter of your mind re-garding the procuring of peace and the alleviation of sufferings consequent upon the war.

Recalling with keen joy the pleasant memories left Us after Our unforgettable visit to your great nation, and living over again the sincere pleasure that personal acquaintance with Your Excellency brought Us, We express in turn Our hearty good wishes, with a most fervent prayer for the prosperity of Your Excellency and of all the people of the United States.

PIUS PP. XII

Given at Rome, at St. Peter's, the 7th day of January, 1940, the First Year of Our Pontificate.

The Dark Days
of 1940

EXPLANATORY NOTE

The four messages (III-VI) in this group relate to the first visit to Rome of the President's Personal Representative to the Pope. That visit lasted from February 27 to August 22, 1940.

Message No. III is the text of a handwritten letter from President Roosevelt to His Holiness, which I presented at my first audience. Message No. IV is the Pope's reply, handed to me for transmission to the President on March 16, 1940.

By that time, conversations with His Holiness and with various foreign officials at the Vatican had confirmed the view that there was no hope of re-establishing peace. Any effort of mediation by neutral states would be untimely and would surely be rebuffed by the Axis Governments, whose position currently was wholly favorable to their ambitions. Under Secretary of State Sumner Welles was arriving at the same conclusion from the direct conversations he was then having with heads of governments in Europe. The message of His Holiness to the President was accordingly written in conditions filled with depression and foreboding.

Since the Government of Italy under Mussolini was just then committing itself to early action against France and Great Britain,— a decision being indicated by numerous reports and activities,—the only possibility that remained of keeping the war from spreading in the Mediterranean area lay in an appeal to him. It was evident that if any such appeal could persuade Mussolini to remain a non-billigerent, it must come from the President or His Holiness. In these circumstances, the President appealed immediately to Mussolini, and when unsuccessful, appealed again.

By mid-April, both the President and the Pope felt that the strongest possible urging was imperative. This action toward the same objective was undertaken promptly with prior arrangement though independently and without consultation as to the substance of the communications. The Pope wrote to Mussolini on April 24. The President addressed his further appeals immediately afterward, and again on May 14. Mussolini, however, believing that Italy was imprisoned in the Mediterranean, wanted "windows on the Atlantic on the one hand and the Red Sea and the Indian Ocean on the other." The appeals were summarily rejected.

Meanwhile, on April 9, German forces invaded Denmark and Norway and, on May 9, Belgium, Luxembourg and The Netherlands. By May 30, British forces began to evacuate Dunkirk and France confronted imminent disastrous defeat. On a schedule known six weeks in advance, undeterred to the end by the far-sighted arguments that had been made to him, Mussolini on June 10 led Italy into war against France and Britain. France surrendered to Germany on June 22 and to Italy on June 24. Britain fought on under heavy attack from the air and on the seas—with her weakness desperately concealed, and with her stamina fortified by immediate threat to her survival.

As these events were occurring, the President condemned the new aggressions. His Holiness wrote messages of sympathy to the Low Countries. A crucial stage had been reached. The strongest efforts to prevent the spread of war had failed.

There remained for action at the moment only two constructive lines of work. To provide for relief of suffering was the first. In Poland, where hostilities had ceased, the plight of millions of people had become tragic, and His Holiness expressed anxiety over the failure of all relief efforts so far. Elsewhere in the active combat areas distress was mounting but the possibilities of relief were as yet scant. In this field the United States Government, lacking controls over organized relief efforts aside from those of the American Red Cross, could only encourage action by others. President Roosevelt asked me in July to convey to His Holiness his hopes that maximum relief could be extended to all the stricken civilian populations, and that relief agencies would be encouraged to coordinate their activities as effectively as possible.

The second field of work was to consider, as and when developing thought might warrant, the bases of an enduring peace. The altered circumstances of the war and the resulting confusion as to the future suggested, however, the need of consultation at home before proceeding *further. A recurrence of ill health on my part also rendered return advisable.*

I took my departure on August 22, carrying to the President a letter from His Holiness (Message No. V) reflecting his continuing faith as to the future despite the discouragements of the hour. Following my report to the President, the President wrote to His Holiness on October 1 (Message No. VI) expressing his own firm intention not to abandon, despite the grim outlook, the search for the way to a truly peaceful world order.—M.C.T.

III

Letter from President Roosevelt to His Holiness

FEBRUARY 14, 1940

Your Holiness:

In my letter of December 23, 1939 I had the honor to suggest that it would give me great satisfaction to send to You my own representative in order that our parallel endeavors for peace and the alleviation of suffering might be assisted. Your Holiness was good enough to reply that the choice of Mr. Myron C. Taylor as my representative was acceptable and that You would receive him.

I am entrusting this special mission to Mr. Taylor who is a very old friend of mine, and in whom I repose the utmost confidence. His humanitarian efforts in behalf of those whom political disruption has rendered homeless are well known to Your Holiness. I shall be happy to feel that he may be the channel of communications for any views You and I may wish to exchange in the interest of concord among the peoples of the world.

I am asking Mr. Taylor to convey my cordial greetings to You, my old and good friend, and my sincere hope that the common ideals of religion and humanity itself can have united expression for the re-establishment of a more permanent peace on the foundations of freedom and an assurance of life and integrity of all nations under God.

Cordially Your friend,

FRANKLIN D. ROOSEVELT

IV

Reply of His Holiness to President Roosevelt

MARCH 16, 1940

Your Excellency:

The pleasure which was Ours on the twenty-seventh day of February as We received in Solemn Audience the Representative of Your Excellency was enhanced by the autograph letter which he bore from you and placed into Our hands. We are sincerely grateful for this further evidence of your solicitude for the restoration of peace among nations now estranged as well as for the expressions of cordial greeting which you have been pleased to use in Our regard.

We confess to have been sensibly affected as We beheld before Us your own Representative come upon a noble mission of peace and healing, to seek with Us ways and means of giving back to a warring world its rightful heritage of concord and the freedom to pursue in justice and tranquility its temporal and eternal happiness. In a moment of universal travail, when hope contends with fear in the souls of so many millions of men, We have been greatly encouraged by the vision of new possibilities of beneficent action opened up to us through the presence near Us of your distinguished Representative. Since the obligations of Christian charity towards the needy and the dispossessed have ever constituted a prior claim upon Our affections and resources as they have upon those of Our Predecessors, it is with particular satisfaction that We welcome Your Excellency's endeavors for the alleviation of suffering. Our contemporaries follow with their heartfelt prayers, and posterity will hold in honored memory, all those who, undeterred by immense difficulties, dedicate themselves to the sacred task of

33

staunching the flow of youthful blood upon the fields of battle, and to the comforting of civilian victims despoiled and afflicted by the cruel conditions of our day. Blessed, indeed, are the peacemakers.

And although one who with discerning eye surveys the present international scene can have no illusions as to the magnitude of the role which has been undertaken, We are convinced that it is in the interest of all that We should go forward with Our labors to the end that the days of grievous trial be shortened, preparing and straightening the way, levelling the mountains of anger which bar the road to understanding and filling up the valleys of distrust and suspicion which divide man from man and nation from nation. Thus may We hope that the natural law, graven by the Creator on the hearts of men, may soon, as it must ultimately, prevail as the universal rule of human conduct over arbitrary whim and sordid interest which here and there have usurped its place, and that in consequence the rising generation may be saved from the moral illiteracy with which they are threatened. And thus, when all shall have come finally to realize that violence is futile and that hatred is a sterile force, a wearied world may rejoice in a peace builded upon the solid foundation of justice and firmly held together by the bonds of fraternal charity.

We renew to Your Excellency the expression of Our gratitude for your greeting while, in the light of happy remembrance, We pray for your continued well-being and for that of the American people.

PIUS PP. XII

Given at Rome, from St. Peter's, the 16th day of
March, 1940, the Second Year of Our Pontificate.

V

Letter from His Holiness to President Roosevelt

Your Excellency:

The return to the United States of Your Excellency's Personal Representative to Us, for the purpose of recruiting in the home-land the forces so generously spent in the fulfilment of his noble mission, affords Us a welcome opportunity of sending you Our cordial greetings, and of reiterating Our appreciation for the presence of Your Envoy near Us. In the light of experience, We now have further and ampler proof of the wisdom which inspired Your Excellency to despatch your Representative to Us, as We also have cause to rejoice at the felicity of choice which led you to entrust this important post to the Honorable Myron C. Taylor.

These first months of the mission have occasioned Us great satisfaction and, in spite of the dark forebodings of the hour, We express Our hope in a future which shall see the re-establishment of a general and enduring peace. Although the horrors of the war increase and Our sorrow deepens with every passing day, We are redoubling Our prayers and Our endeavors to find a practicable way to such a peace as will bear within it the promise of permanency, and free men from the heavy incubus of insecurity and of perpetual alarms. In Our unceasing search for that peace which will be no longer, as so often in the past, a parenthesis of exhaustion between two phases of conflict, but rather, by the grace of God, a golden era of Christian concord dedicated to the spiritual and material improvement of humanity, We feel a distinct sense of comfort in the thought that We shall not be without the powerful support of the President of the United States.

It is therefore with heartfelt good will that We again assure Your Excellency of Our prayers for your continued health and happiness and for the prosperity and progress of the American people.

PIUS PP. XII

Given at Rome, from St. Peter's, the 22nd day of August, 1940, the Second Year of Our Pontificate.

VI

Reply of President Roosevelt to His Holiness

Your Holiness,

Upon his return to the United States, Mr. Myron C. Taylor duly delivered to me Your message of August twenty-second and I am deeply gratified by Your Holiness' expression of satisfaction concerning Mr. Taylor's mission.

Particular note has been taken of the assurance of Your Holiness' continuing efforts to find the way to a peace which bears promise not only of permanency, but also of freedom from perpetual alarm and opportunity for the spiritual and material improvement of humanity. It seems imperative that this search shall not be abandoned, no matter how deep may be the shadow of the present strife. It is equally necessary to realize that peace as Your Holiness conceives it must be based upon the re-establishment of Christian law and doctrine as the guiding principles which govern the relations of free men and free nations. The spiritual freedom and political independence which alone make possible this rebuilding of the structure of peace thus become a necessary part of our common goal. In the search of it, the Government and people of the United States are glad to lend their sympathy and to devote their efforts.

May I assure Your Holiness of my profound appreciation of the reception accorded to Mr. Taylor and of Your message of good will.

May I also take this occasion to send to Your Holiness my very deep personal good wishes and to express my hope and wish for Your continued good health. The whole world needs You in its search for peace and good will.

Faithfully yours,

FRANKLIN DELANO ROOSEVELT

*"The Seekers of Light
and the
Seekers of Peace"*

EXPLANATORY NOTE

The next occasion for an exchange of messages was President Roosevelt's re-election in November, 1940. The Pope's message of congratulation, dated December 20, and the President's reply on March 3, 1941, reflected the profound developments which occurred in the course of the war during the last few months of the year 1940 and the early months of 1941.

Great Britain, standing almost alone, continued to sustain the violence of full German attack. The United States had extended to her the help of fifty destroyers in return for leases of needed bases in the North Atlantic and the Caribbean.

Germany, Italy and Japan had entered into a ten-year military pact. The Baltic states of Estonia, Latvia and Lithuania, and the eastern part of Rumania had been incorporated into the Soviet Union. France under the Vichy regime had broken with Britain on the issue of preserving the French fleet from enemy use, and had then undertaken fuller cooperation with Nazi Germany.

The war began to spread into the Balkans with Italy's attack on Greece and with preparatory moves by Germany after the failure of plans to crush Britain by September, 1940. Japan created new tensions in the Pacific with repeated indications of military interest in Thailand and other parts of Asia and the Southern Pacific, and of political hostility to American embargoes on military materials.

United States defenses were being strengthened on a widening scale, and manpower was being trained. At last, in crucial crisis, the democracies were developing an arsenal of the instruments vital to their continuance as free peoples.

The Pope's letter of congratulation (Message No. VII) conveyed prayerful encouragement to continue to strive for universal order, justice and peace. President Roosevelt responded (Message No. VIII) with the hope that lasting concord between men and nations would again be established through friendly association among all who sought peace, stressing anew that an enduring peace must be founded upon Christian principles and upon freedom from the threat of aggression.—M.C.T.

VII

Letter from His Holiness to President Roosevelt

DECEMBER 20, 1940

His Excellency Franklin D. Roosevelt
President of the United States of America
Washington, D. C.

In being elected for a third term to the Presidency of the United States of America, at a time of such grave moment for the life of nations, Your Excellency has received from your country a singular proof of confidence.

The personal relations had with Your Excellency on the occasion of Our visit to the United States, when We were Cardinal Secretary of State to the late lamented Supreme Pontiff, and the gracious reception you extended to Us, put Us in the way to appreciate your generous spirit; and today, while We offer you congratulations, We pray Almighty God to guide your mind and heart in the noble and arduous task of leading a free and vigorous people for the greater stability of universal order, justice and peace.

A tangible proof of these generous dispositions We have had in your sending His Excellency Mr. Myron Taylor to Us, as your Personal Representative with rank of Ambassador Extraordinary. Special circumstances have interrupted his presence with Us; but We like to hope that the plan for the attainment of those high ideals you had in mind may yet be realized.

Indeed, We are not unaware of the efforts which you made to prevent the catastrophic struggle that is heaping up ruin and sorrow for a great part of the Old World; and in Our paternal solicitude for suffering humanity there is nothing We desire more ardently than to see true peace return at long last among

43

peoples, who have been too long and too painfully stricken and afflicted:—that true peace, We mean, that will adjust all wrongs, that will recognize with well-judged equity the vital necessities of all, and thus mark for the world the beginning of a new era of tranquility, collaboration and progress among peoples under the longed-for reign of Christian justice and charity.

While We renew the expression of Our good wishes for you personally and for the nation over which you preside, We invoke on both an abundance of God's blessings.

PIUS PP. XII

Given at Rome, from the Palace of the Vatican, the twentieth day of December, 1940, the Second Year of Our Pontificate.

VIII

Reply of President Roosevelt to His Holiness

MARCH 3, 1941

Your Holiness:

Your Holiness has been good enough to send me a message upon the occasion of my re-election to the Presidency of the United States of America and to recall the cordial relations I had with Your Holiness when, as Cardinal Secretary of State, You visited this country.

I take this occasion not only to express my profound appreciation of Your message but to reiterate the hope that through friendly association between the seekers of light and the seekers of peace everywhere a firm basis of lasting concord between men and nations can be established throughout the world once again. Only when the principles of Christianity and the right of all peoples to live free from the threat of external aggression are established can that peace which Your Holiness and I so ardently desire be found.

To my deep regret Mr. Myron Taylor has been obliged to interrupt his mission in Italy but I hope that his health may soon be sufficiently restored to enable him to return to Rome.

Believe me, with the assurances of my highest regard,

Yours very sincerely,

FRANKLIN DELANO ROOSEVELT

Easter—April, 1941

EXPLANATORY NOTE

Eastertide, 1941, provided the next occasion for an exchange of messages. By that time, the war had moved into all parts of southeastern Europe and its repercussions began sharply to affect parts of the Near and Middle East. The Axis leaders continued to possess all initiative of action, and their success had been hampered seriously only in Greece, and denied beyond the coasts of the continent. Hitler decided to attack the Soviet Union—forewarning of which, when intelligence was reported in January and in March to the American Government, was promptly communicated to the Soviet Government.

But, darkening as the prospect was, determined resistance continued and the necessary means of defense were being provided increasingly. The President on January 6 had recommended, and in a few weeks the Congress had approved in the interest of our own security, the passage of legislation to lend-lease supplies and materials to nations defending themselves from aggression.

At the same time the President declared that for a secure future, America looked forward to a world founded upon four essential freedoms—freedom of speech and expression, freedom of religion, freedom from want, and freedom from fear. In his Easter greeting to His Holiness (Message No. IX), he further explained his views on these freedoms. This message reflected the President's deep reliance upon the moral sense of humanity, and his faith that the freedoms essential to a moral world order were attainable.

As he had said in an address a year earlier:

"Today we seek a moral basis for peace. It cannot be a real peace if it fails to recognize brotherhood. It cannot be a lasting peace if the fruit of it is oppression, or starvation, or cruelty, or human life dominated by armed camps. It cannot be a sound peace if small nations must live in fear of powerful neighbors. It cannot be a moral peace if freedom from invasion is sold for tribute. It cannot be an intelligent peace if it denies free passage

*to that knowledge of those ideals which permit men to find com-
mon ground. It cannot be a righteous peace if worship of God
is denied."*

*The message from the Pope replying immediately to the President
(Message No. X) was written in sadness over the human misery and
the devastation brought by the spreading conflict in the spring of 1941.
Its words reflected in turn the unflagging will of His Holiness then,
and constantly despite all obstacles, to persevere in efforts to ameliorate
the suffering during the war and to plead to the thought and conscience
of the world for a true peace. These Easter messages bore eloquent
testimony to the developing harmony of views concerning the fundamental goals of the peace toward which the President and Pope Pius
XII were each so firmly striving.—*M.C.T.

IX

Message from President Roosevelt to His Holiness

[TELEGRAM] EASTER—APRIL, 1941

His Holiness Pope Pius XII
Vatican City

Your Holiness:

I send You my most cordial greetings at Easter. The time is admittedly full of pain and danger. Yet from all parts of the world messages reach me which justify the high hope that the light of the world is being rekindled. These messages make it plain that courageous spirits are everywhere arising above fear, and that ever-increasing numbers of brave souls refuse to be separated from their Father in Heaven or from their brothers on earth by force or by falsehoods or by fear. So long as the human spirit is undefeated, the great elementary human freedoms will inevitably be triumphant. Here in the United States we believe that freedom of worship is the first and greatest need of us all. For that reason we have exerted all of our influence against religious persecutions, which for the first time in centuries again threaten the brotherhood of man in many parts of the world. We have likewise sought freedom of information so that no conqueror can enslave men's minds or prevent them from finding their way to the truth. We have set our minds to attaining freedom from fear, so that no man, no family, no nation, need live perpetually under the shadow of danger from bombs, invasion, and ensuing devastation. And we propose to forward the cause of freedom from want by direct relief where this is possible and necessary and by so improving the economic processes of life that children may be born and families may be reared in safety and comfort. I am convinced that such a rebirth of the moral sense of humanity can muster a force infinitely greater than that of a transient parade of arms with nothing behind it save the confusion and corruption of a group which has lost all spiritual values, and solely lust for power. Only the most short-sighted of statesmen can fail to see this. Let me include in my greetings this Easter not merely a sense of hope which reaches me from many lands, but also my considered conviction that these great freedoms are once more attainable. Their achievement only awaits the resolute action of men who answer bravely the clear call to their ancient fidelity to the Lord and to their fellowmen.

FRANKLIN D. ROOSEVELT

X

Message from His Holiness to President Roosevelt

[TELEGRAM] EASTER—APRIL, 1941

His Excellency Franklin D. Roosevelt
President of the United States of America
Washington, D. C.

We thank Your Excellency for the greetings which you have so kindly sent Us for Easter. In these festive days of joyful commemoration Our heart is particularly saddened by the thought of the massacre and widespread devastation which the present conflict is leaving in its wake. In the name of human civilization and above all inspired by that divine love brought to man by the Redeemer We have not failed and We shall not fail to do everything possible to alleviate the sufferings of those in need and in carrying out this beneficent work of charity We have found unbounded sympathy and generous cooperation among Our beloved children of the United States. Not content with this We have felt and We feel it Our duty to raise Our voice, the voice of a Father not moved by any earthly interests but animated only by a desire for the common good of all, in a plea for a peace that will be genuine, just, honorable, and lasting; a peace that will respect individuals, families and nations and safeguard their rights to life, to a reasonable liberty, to a conscientious and fervent practice of religion, to true progress, and to an equitable participation in the riches which providence has distributed with largess over the earth; a peace whose spirit and provisions will tend to revitalize and revigorate through new and enlightened organization the true spirit of brotherhood among men today so tragically alienated one from another. With these hopes which find expression in Our

53

fervent prayer to the Divine Goodness We are happy in turn to assure Your Excellency at this Eastertide of Our good wishes not only for your personal welfare but also for the prosperity of the great and cherished people of the United States.

PIUS PP. XII

Assistance to the Soviet Union

EXPLANATORY NOTE

Two events of profound significance occurred during the summer of 1941. The first was the German attack on the Soviet Union in June. The second was the meeting, in August, of President Roosevelt and Prime Minister Winston Churchill, which gave rise to their joint declaration known as the "Atlantic Charter".

The first event immediately posed the problem of whether or not aid should be given to the Soviet Union, reeling in retreat under the violence of the Nazi onslaught. By reason of the Communist philosophy of the Soviet Government, the answer to that problem involved the fundamental attitudes of most of the world's peoples and institutions regarding some of the most treasured values and aspirations of human society which Communism had rejected. The issue as it swiftly emerged, however, was in stark fact whether Hitler's intended conquest of Russia, so essential to the success of his plans for putting the world under domination of a Nazi order in which democracy could not survive, would be thwarted or not.

The Government and people of the United States,—as did the Government and people of Great Britain,—immediately determined to give every practicable form of assistance—not to Communism, alien alike to America's and Britain's faith and way of life, but toward preventing Nazi Germany from conquering the Russian people and thus securing the wheat and oil and other means necessary to carry on further aggression. To this measured decision was added, as time went on, an increasing admiration for the Russian people who despite immense suffering fought tenaciously in defense of their homeland.

A problem so posed and so answered was one not only for governments and nations but for all churches. This was true in a special way for Americans of Catholic faith, who were aware of the encyclical issued by Pope Pius XI in 1922 which contained a broad condemnation of atheistic communism and forbade collaboration with it, while expressing compassion for the suffering and oppression of the Russian people. Consequently, clarifications of American feeling and opinion to

His Holiness regarding aid to the Soviet Union and of the views of His Holiness in the same regard, were desirable. The next exchange of views between the President and His Holiness was directed to that purpose and was the occasion of my second visit to Rome.

The opportunity to exchange views in connection with the Atlantic Charter also made a visit desirable. That document contained, as is well known, eight far-reaching statements of policy and common principles on which its authors based their hope for a better future.

Since that joint declaration represented a substantial advance over the views as to the bases of future peace which had already been discussed with the Pope, the President wished me to ascertain whether He found its views in harmony with His own. He hoped that if the Charter commended itself, as he believed it would, the Pope would make His impressions known to the world.

The President's letter of September 3 (Message No. XI) was handed to His Holiness in audience on September 9.

His Holiness confirmed the view that the Holy See condemned atheistic communism and Soviet practices regarding individual liberty, but that, as at all times, the Holy See continued to regard the Russian people with paternal affection. This view was stated in an allocution immediately thereafter and again in His Holiness' Christmas Eve broadcast the same year.

While the freedom of conscience and religious worship which was assured to the Russian people in Article 124 of the Constitution of the U.S.S.R. was in practice not honored in many essential respects, the President had the hope that religious freedom would ultimately be fully respected. This hope was fortified at that time by the more favorable official Soviet attitude toward religious worship being expressed currently in the Soviet press and in an address by the Soviet Ambassador in London. Nevertheless, reports of conditions continued to cast doubt on whether improvement was progressing, and so this hope necessarily had to continue to rest in the slow processes of time.

A number of President Roosevelt's views relating to the Atlantic Charter were conveyed in the same discussions. The President believed *that accomplishment of disarmament would take many years. The peace-loving nations must be able by police power to prevent aggression. Peaceful self-determination—both territorial and political—was a continuing process which worked toward elimination of war. He depended much upon freedom to trade to contribute to prosperity generally. In the existing world confusion the principle of trusteeship—unselfish service—might well be utilized more widely in international affairs than solely in regard to mandates as in the past. Freedom of religion and freedom of expression were necessary in every aspect of the future peace and called for spiritual leadership in opposition to the pagan views and objectives of the Axis powers.*

These views were received with much pleasure by the Pope. The notable address by the Pope on the following Christmas, concerning the essential conditions of world order under moral law, reflected still further growth of harmony of views on the bases of future world peace.

The letter of His Holiness, dated September 20 (Message No. XII), together with His views corresponding to the foregoing, were carried to the President upon my return.—M.C.T.

XI

Letter from President Roosevelt to His Holiness

SEPTEMBER 3, 1941

Your Holiness:

At my request, Mr. Myron Taylor will discuss with Your Holiness certain matters with regard to which I am very desirous that he explain my feelings and American opinion. These are matters in regard to which I feel very strongly.

The first of these relates to the problem of the attitude of the Russian Government and the Russian people toward religion. In so far as I am informed, churches in Russia are open. I believe there is a real possibility that Russia may as a result of the present conflict recognize freedom of religion in Russia, although, of course, without recognition of any official intervention on the part of any church in education or political matters within Russia. I feel that if this can be accomplished it will put the possibility of the restoration of real religious liberty in Russia on a much better footing than religious freedom is in Germany today.

There are in the United States many people in *all* churches who have the feeling that Russia is governed completely by a communistic form of society. In my opinion, the fact is that Russia is governed by a dictatorship, as rigid in its manner of being as is the dictatorship in Germany. I believe, however, that this Russian dictatorship is less dangerous to the safety of other nations than is the German form of dictatorship. The only weapon which the Russian dictatorship uses outside of its own borders is communist propaganda which I, of course, recognize has in the past been utilized for the purpose of breaking down the form of government in other countries, religious belief, et cetera. Germany, however, not only has utilized, but is utilizing, this kind of propaganda as well and has also under-taken the employment of every form of military aggression out-side of its borders for the purpose of world conquest by force of arms and by force of propaganda. I believe that the survival of Russia is less dangerous to religion, to the church as such, and to humanity in general than would be the survival of the German form of dictatorship. Furthermore, it is my belief that the leaders of all churches in the United States should recognize these facts clearly and should not close their eyes to these basic questions and by their present attitude on this question directly assist Germany in her present objectives.

Bearing in mind the common desire which Your Holiness and I share that a firm basis for lasting concord between men and nations founded on the principles of Christianity can again be established, I have asked Mr. Taylor to explain my feelings in this matter in order that Your Holiness may understand my position in this respect.

Believe me, with the assurances of my highest regard,

Yours very sincerely,

FRANKLIN DELANO ROOSEVELT

XII

Reply of His Holiness to President Roosevelt

SEPTEMBER 20, 1941

Your Excellency:

We have received with satisfaction and pleasure your esteemed letter of September third and we gladly avail Ourselves of the return to Washington of His Excellency Mr. Myron C. Taylor to forward to you this note of cordial acknowledgment.

We learned with gratification of the coming of your Personal Representative, who has always been a devoted and conscientious bearer of tidings from Your Excellency and who remains a welcome link between you and Us.

Mr. Taylor has called upon Us several times and We have been very happy to receive him on each occasion. He has presented to Us a full exposition of those matters which are uppermost in the mind of Your Excellency at the present time and he has graciously informed Us of your personal feelings and of the general sentiment of your people. We, in turn, have expressed to Mr. Taylor Our point of view regarding the important matters which were dealt with in our conversations. He has assured Us that, upon his return to Washington, he will give Your Excellency an accurate report in this regard.

It is Our constant prayer and sincere hope that Almighty God may hasten the day when men and nations now at war will enjoy the blessings of a true and enduring peace—a peace in which We confidently foresee embodied those fundamental Christian principles, whose application can assure the victory of love over hate, right over might, justice over egoism, and in which the search for eternal values will prevail over the quest for merely temporal goods. Meanwhile We find Ourselves, however, face to face with the appalling and heart-sickening consequences of modern warfare. In these tragic circumstances We are endeavoring, with all the forces at Our disposal, to bring material and spiritual comfort to countless thousands who are numbered amongst the innocent and helpless victims. We should like, on this occasion, to express to Your Excellency Our cordial appreciation of the magnificent assistance which the American people have given, and continue to offer, in this mission of mercy. They are, indeed, demonstrating once again a charitable understanding of the needs of their suffering fellow-men and a noble desire to alleviate their misery.

In reassuring you of Our ceaseless and untiring efforts in the cause of peace, We renew to Your Excellency the expression of Our heartfelt good wishes, with a fervent prayer for the personal welfare of Your Excellency and for the prosperity of the cherished people of the United States.

PIUS PP. XII

From the Vatican,
September 20th, 1941.

America At War

EXPLANATORY NOTE

A year elapsed before the next exchange of messages. In the early months of this interval, American relations with Japan progressively became more tense, though negotiations for adjustment of the gravely deepening crisis in the Far East proceeded almost continuously. On December 7, 1941, by surprise attack at Pearl Harbor, war came to the United States in the Pacific. Within four days, by the declarations of war on the United States by Germany and Italy, the war at last girded the entire globe.

The ultimate issue whether the philosophy of militarism and aggression or the philosophy of peaceful democracy would have the opportunity to be conferred by victory to mold the world's future now rested in the arbitrament of battle throughout all continents and on all seas. Almost no neutrals remained in the world, but only enemy or ally. The enemy states possessed the preponderance of ready force. The states allied in war immediately joined together in a Declaration by United Nations to cooperate in the prosecution of the conflict and not to make a separate armistice or peace with the enemies.

The developments of the war during the spring and summer of 1942 are still vivid in the memory of all. These were months of retreat, of organization of plans and forces, of costly decision as to what forces were "expendable". They were months when courage and faith in ultimate victory were tested by multiplied defeats and the tolls of military campaigns.

Yet, as the United States took up the gage of war, peace no less than victory was in the mind of President Roosevelt. "We shall win this war", he wrote, "and in victory we shall seek not vengeance but the establishment of an international order in which the Spirit of Christ shall rule the hearts of men and of nations."

By September 1, 1942 it appeared that the Italian Government would permit transit of the President's Personal Representative through the Kingdom of Italy. The President at once wrote to His Holiness (Message No. XIII) to initiate my third visit. This letter was pre-

sented in audience on September 19. As proposed by the President, an explanation was at once made as to America's views concerning the war, and beyond, along the following lines:

The Japanese attack had consolidated the American people into a single entity to win the war. America would choose its own time and place to bring its forces to bear. Meanwhile we believed Russia would not surrender even though pressed at this time to the limit of strength. The first principal adversary to be defeated would be Germany, and then in due course, and in America's own way, Japan.

America's interest was in defense of an ideal of government and a way of life for itself and for mankind. It sought no political, financial or territorial aggrandisement. It was moving and would move in harmony with all those who would defend human rights and justice under the moral law. America had no hatred for the Italian people. Even yet it was not too late for Italy's people to find their eventual position determined by their conduct henceforth. Nor did America hate the German people though our feeling was affected by apprehension that they upheld the aggressions of their leaders.

The United States was determined to carry through until complete victory had been won. The American people were united in that determination regardless of any normal differences of interest or belief among them. No indecisive or compromised victory would suffice; it would signify a partial victory for the Axis and could only lead to later resumption of conflict. After full victory, a just and lasting peace must be made. Until victory, no peace was possible. The war aims of the United States were peace aims—aims known to His Holiness and to the world.

These reflections met with happy response from His Holiness. At my request, He later provided for the information of the President a copy of a personal memorandum in which He had set forth His views to me in regard to several of these vital matters.

The memorandum envisaged an eventual peace worthy of man's personal dignity and of his high destiny, a peace which took into consideration the vital needs of all nations and which bore within itself the seeds of longevity. A first requisite was that the relations between gov-

ernments and their people, and between all governments and peoples, must be based on the fulfillment of contracts, on the observance of justice and law tempered by Christian charity and brotherly love, and on reverence for the dignity of the human person and respect for religious convictions. The worship of God must again exercise its due influence in individual and national life. The Pope again stated, as in earlier public utterances, that certain principles of right and justice have their foundation deep in the moral order of the universe, and that on such principles there can never be compromise. He was greatly heartened to know that the peace aims of the United States fully recognized these basic moral principles. These principles would unswervingly point the direction of His own path of duty.

Occasion was taken, with the approval of the President and Secretary Hull, to describe in general terms the significant efforts being made by the Advisory Committee on Post-War Foreign Policy, which had been established early in the preceding February, and in the work of which I was participating. This Committee, under Secretary Hull's Chairmanship and with participation by members of the public and of the Congress and by officials, was intensively engaged in exploring post-war problems with a view to making recommendations to the President. Its fields of work concerned transitional problems of relief, re-establishment of order, and reconstruction, as well as all the complex and far-reaching aspects of post-war international security; long-range political, territorial, and economic problems; and international organization. No conclusions had as yet been drawn and none would be until long and serious study had been given to the problems.

While the Pope, in accord with the traditional policy of the Holy See to abstain from participating in controversial problems between states outside the spiritual sphere, commented upon this information only as to its bearing upon the establishment of just and enduring peace, He expressed gratification that the application of American peace aims had become so quickly the subject of responsible preparations.

When I took leave His Holiness handed to me the letter addressed by Him to President Roosevelt under date of September 25 (Message

No. XIV) manifesting confidence that a new spirit of collaboration among men and nations would unite men after the war, and conveying to the President,—now as leader not of a neutral but of a belligerent state,—His desire for continuance of parallel endeavors for the alleviation of suffering and for peace.—M.C.T.

XIII

Letter from President Roosevelt to His Holiness

SEPTEMBER 3, 1942

Your Holiness:

I am very happy that Mr. Myron C. Taylor is going back to the Vatican to see You and that apparently the passage has been assured.

He will tell You of all that has gone on in America since he last saw You, and he will tell You how important I believe it to be that we maintain close contacts and close understandings.

I well know what great difficulties surround You and I know that You are praying for us in the United States just as You are praying for all humanity.

I hope especially that Your health is good and that You will take care of Yourself—for we all need You in this critical time.

With my warm regards,

Faithfully Yours,

FRANKLIN DELANO ROOSEVELT

XIV

Reply of His Holiness to President Roosevelt

SEPTEMBER 25, 1942

Your Excellency:

Once again We have welcomed with especial satisfaction your Personal Representative, His Excellency Mr. Myron C. Taylor, whose untiring and devoted efforts serve so effectively to foster the relations between Your Excellency and Us.

We continue to strive, with every means at Our disposal, for the foundation of a world order that will have as its basis the fundamental principles of justice and charity, and it is Our confident prayer that in the post-war world men and nations may unite in a new spirit of understanding and collaboration. As Your Excellency has remarked, Our labors for the alleviation of suffering and for peace encounter obstacles and difficulties, but We place Our trust in God and are confident that We shall enjoy the understanding collaboration of all good people.

In renewing to Your Excellency the expression of Our good wishes, We assure you of Our fervent prayers for your personal welfare and for that of the people of the United States of America.

PIUS PP. XII

From the Vatican,
September 25, 1942.

The Turning Point
of the War

EXPLANATORY NOTE

The three months that passed between the President's receipt of the reply dated September 25, 1942, and his next message (No. XV) were, in many ways, the most crucial months of the war. In retrospect, the developments which occurred then marked, though tentatively and with reverses still to come, the decisive turn in the trend of world events. American armies with the cooperation of British forces landed in North Africa in a campaign attended by immediate successes toward freeing North Africa from Axis forces. A Soviet offensive in the area of Stalingrad and another in the Caucasus evidenced that reserve of power and determination which were capable at last of checking the forward thrust of Nazi forces on the Eastern Front. And in the Pacific, at the farthest point of Japanese advance, Japan's greatest naval effort to re-capture Guadalcanal failed. The ebb of the tide of aggressive expansion by the Axis had set in.

The message from President Roosevelt to His Holiness dated December 31, 1942 was written as this crucial moment in the war was reached. With a profound sense of the responsibility that his leadership conferred, the President wrote in deep feeling of the necessity to banish war as an instrument of national policy and to replace it by an intelligent system to achieve unbroken peace.

Responding in the same spirit of complete dedication to duty in days of violent crisis, January 5, 1943 (Message No. XVI), His Holiness expressed His longing for the return of peace and His readiness to collaborate in fullest measure whenever well-founded hope would appear. Meanwhile He was seeking to relieve the suffering of prisoners of war, of the families of soldiers, and of the millions of men, women and children who were being subjected to privation, and to keep prayerful watch on the matters of peace.

The efforts to provide relief to which the Pope referred encompassed, among many others, the establishment of arrangements for exchange of information concerning prisoners of war in Eastern Europe, which encountered difficulties that largely remained unresolved, and for communi-

cation of news between prisoners of war in other theaters of war and their families at home, which fortunately had a substantial degree of success. Efforts also were made successfully toward preventing the deportation from Italy of non-Italian and especially Yugoslav Jews to a doomed fate in Poland; and toward ameliorating the conditions of Yugoslav internees in the Italian concentration camp on the island of Arbe. Assistance to ease the plight of innumerable individuals and many groups was being extended wherever conditions permitted.—M.C.T.

XV

Message from President Roosevelt to His Holiness

Your Holiness:

As the Christmas season once more sheds its beatific influence upon the world, I send my greetings and the expression of my earnest hope for the continued health and well-being of Your Holiness. In past years our voices have jointly and severally been raised in behalf of the maintenance of peace. Our appeals have unfortunately fallen upon deaf ears.

We face the new year now upon us with the task to uphold by our deeds and to fulfill in our day the obligations civilization has laid upon us to crush those who refuse to honor the basic principles of Christian conduct. In this spirit we gird ourselves to the task, free from designs upon our neighbors and moved by ideals of humanity, charity and justice under moral law. This consecration knows no limits of effort or sacrifice by our people. Your recent letter brought to me by my Personal Representative has given me the greatest pleasure, as did also a memorandum by Your Holiness in response to his explanation of the position and objectives of this Government and people and of their accomplishments and preparations for defensive war. In modern times war is an especially ominous word. The present war has developed on a world-wide scale, spreading into the most remote places. Its very spread clearly shows that it must be banished as an instrument of national policy by every nation, that it must be replaced by an intelligent system evolved from the skill and courage of those who are entrusted with leadership to find other ways to adjust disputes and to achieve continual peace.

It has given me the greatest satisfaction and I am greatly heartened again to receive from Your Holiness such positive assurances which will enable us to continue our efforts along parallel lines. May I take advantage of this opportunity to re- iterate the hope that Your Holiness may continue in good health and spirit and that these tragic times may soon come to an end.

FRANKLIN D. ROOSEVELT

XVI

Reply of His Holiness to President Roosevelt

JANUARY 5, 1943

Your Excellency:

The greetings and good wishes which Your Excellency has so kindly extended to Us for the holy season of Christmas have been a source of particular pleasure to Us.

Our heart, too, is saddened by the thought that once again the serene light that radiates from Bethlehem shines upon a world troubled and ensanguined by the war.

We derive comfort, however, from the certainty that, in homage to the duty which Our universal paternity and the very feeling of humanity imposed upon Us, We have not spared Ourselves in Our efforts as Your Excellency has so courteously recalled—in order, first of all, that the world might continue to enjoy the inestimable benefits of peace and, later, that the conflagration, once it had broken out, might not spread to other countries.

And now, as the clash of arms sombrely resounds from hemisphere to hemisphere, it remains for Us only to hasten, with longing desire, the return of peace and, above all, to implore it of God through the persevering insistence of prayer, ready always to offer Our fullest collaboration when, through the overhanging clouds of sorrow and destruction, there may shine upon this war-torn world even a faint ray of encouraging and well-founded hope.

While maintaining this prayerful watch, which, though it adds to Our sorrows, does not diminish Our courage, We are not inactive. Your Excellency is aware of the fact—particularly because you have given Us your support for which We shall be ever grateful—that it is Our undeviating program to do everything in Our power to alleviate the countless sufferings arising from this tragic conflict: sufferings of the prisoners and of the wounded, of families in fear and trembling over the fate of their loved ones, of entire peoples subjected to limitless privations and hardships: sufferings of the aged, of women and children who at a moment's notice find themselves deprived of home and possessions.

For Our part, We shall continue to recall to men's minds, as We have done so many times, from this Rome, Holy City, center of the Catholic world and Our Episcopal See, those higher principles of justice and Christian morality without which there is no salvation, and to draw men's spirits anew towards those sentiments of charity and brotherhood without which there can be no peace.

In the ceaseless furtherance of this, Our program, We feel certain that We may count upon the efficacious comprehension of the noble American people and upon the valid collaboration of Your Excellency.

It is in this spirit that, while extending Our fervent good wishes to Your Excellency, at the beginning of this New Year, We pray to God for the prosperity of Your Excellency and that of the great Nation over which you preside.

PIUS PP. XII

The Invasion of Italy

EXPLANATORY NOTE

The five messages contained in this group relate to the summer months of 1943, in the course of which the Allied offensive moved inexorably toward Italy and, finally, into Italy. The plainly foreseeable invasion of Europe from the south foreshadowed new sufferings for Italian civilians and threat of destruction of treasured monuments of the history, religion and culture of the Western World. In deep anxiety the Pope appealed to the President on May 18, 1943 (Message No. XVII). In moving words reflecting the calls for protection and intercession being made to Him, and expressing His grief and apprehension over what might befall the innocent victims of the struggle and civilization's precious heritage when war would rage over a land filled with cultural and religious buildings and shrines, the Pope pleaded that these be spared.

The President replied (Message No. XVIII) with sympathetic appreciation of the deep feeling of His Holiness. Nevertheless, compelled as leader of a warring nation to prosecute the war with all force against any legitimate military objective, he could only promise that warfare would not be made against civilians or against non-military objectives. Allied aviators had been instructed to prevent bombs from falling on Vatican City.

On July 10 the Allies began the invasion of Sicily. The President at once informed His Holiness (Message No. XIX) of the landing of American and British troops on Italian soil. Though mindful of "the grim duties of war", he reaffirmed that religious institutions would be protected so far as this could be done, and promised that the neutral status of Papal domains would be respected.

The first bombing of Rome occurred as the Pope composed His reply to this message, sent on July 19 (Message No. XX). He had seen its effects,—among them that an ancient cultural and religious sanctuary had been struck by a miscarrying bomb. Speaking from vision above the armed conflict of the nations, He again pressingly pleaded that Italy and especially Rome not be bombed. As a foundation of the peace

85

to be built later, He prayed that not alone human charity, but Christian charity, would be shown in the war.

During the next six weeks Mussolini met Hitler for the last time before his resignation, forced by the Grand Council on July 25. Field Marshal Pietro Badoglio took the reins of government as Premier, and the Facist party was immediately dissolved. The Allied conquest of Sicily was completed on August 17. It was in the midst of these decisive developments—only a few days before the invasion of Italy proper by Allied forces and just before German forces occupied Rome—that His Holiness wrote again (Message No. XXI), making a last appeal that innocent civilians and religious institutions be protected from military actions. At the same time He indicated to the President how greatly His hopes to this end were sustained by the intention expressed by the President in his previous message to act in accord with this plea to the extent humanly possible.

A turbulent period of changes followed Italy's surrender on September 8. Five weeks later that country joined in the war against Germany. The struggle against Nazi forces in Italy continued month after month in the campaigns at the foothold of the Allied troops not far from Rome in the region of Anzio and in central Italy. Many emergency problems arose in the combat zones, and my mission gave such help as it could in meeting them. A number came from the difficulties of distinguishing true fact from false in confusing reports. Sometimes religious buildings were used by the enemy and so made military objectives. Our own forces on occasion requisitioned religious property during the battles. The risk was always present that, despite all care, bombs would strike Vatican City, as happened three times, happily with but minor damage. Beyond these were problems of arrangements to assure civil order and to meet medical and other relief needs in Rome and elsewhere as German forces were driven back.

During the winter, Soviet forces continued to regain vast areas lost earlier. They entered the land of pre-war Poland at the turn of the year and broke into Rumania in the spring of 1944. In the Pacific, Japanese forces were attacked and overwhelmed in island after island, and by May

American forces were at Biak Island, 900 miles from the Philippines.

No less favorable advances were made in United Nations collaboration for peace, beginning with the Declaration of Moscow in October 1943 in which the United States, Great Britain, the Soviet Union and China pledged the continuance of their cooperation in the establishment of the peace. Various decisions were made as to the treatment to be accorded Germany and Japan immediately after their surrender. A United Nations Relief and Rehabilitation Administration was being established, and steps toward permanent international organizations were being taken in fields such as food and agriculture, monetary stabilization, investment and development, and civil aviation. Moreover, the four major nations fighting the Axis were preparing to formulate at Dumbarton Oaks their proposals for a general world organization to maintain international peace and security.

By summer 1944, the cause of the United Nations, both in the war and toward the use of victory for the highest constructive purposes, enjoyed a most hopeful prospect.

*Rome, fortunately not damaged extensively, was liberated on June 4, 1944, and the battles in Italy moved northward. Two days later Allied forces successfully landed in France and swept irresistibly onward to liberate Western Europe. Yet the issue of the titanic struggle in all its theaters in Europe and in the Far East, certain though it appeared, remained far from final decision, and excepting the cooperation among the major nations already pledged, the basic problems of future world peace remained to be solved by necessary agreements and action.—*M.C.T.

XVII

Letter from His Holiness to President Roosevelt

MAY 18, 1943

Your Excellency,

Almost four years have now passed since, in the name of the God the Father of all and with the utmost earnestness at Our command, We appealed (August 24, 1939) to the responsible leaders of peoples to hold back the threatening avalanche of international strife and to settle their differences in the calm, serene atmosphere of mutual understanding. "Nothing was to be lost by peace; everything might be lost by war." And when the awful powers of destruction broke loose and swept over a large part of Europe, though Our Apostolic Office places Us above and beyond all participation in armed conflicts, We did not fail to do what We could to keep out of the war nations not yet involved and to mitigate as far as possible for millions of innocent men, women and children, defenceless against the circumstances in which they have to live, the sorrows and sufferings that would inevitably follow along the constantly widening swath of desolation and death cut by the machines of modern warfare.

The succeeding years unfortunately have seen heart-rending tragedies increase and multiply; yet We have not for that reason, as Our conscience bears witness, given over Our hopes and Our efforts in behalf of the afflicted members of the great human family everywhere. And as the Episcopal See of the Popes is Rome, from where through these long centuries they have ruled the flock entrusted to them by the divine Shepherd of souls, it is natural that amid all the vicissitudes of their complex and chequered history the faithful of Italy should feel themselves bound by more than ordinary ties to this Holy See, and have learned to look to it for protection and comfort especially in hours of crisis.

In such an nour today their pleading voices reach Us carried on their steady confidence that they will not go un-answered. Fathers and mothers, old and young every day are appealing for Our help; and We, whose paternal heart beats in unison with the sufferings and sorrows of all mankind, cannot but respond with the deepest feelings of Our soul to such insistent prayers, lest the poor and humble shall have placed their confidence in Us in vain.

And so very sincerely and confidently We address Our-selves to Your Excellency, sure that no one will recognize more clearly than the Chief Executive of the great American nation the voice of humanity that speaks in these appeals to Us, and the affection of a father that inspires Our response.

The assurance given to Us in 1941 by Your Excellency's esteemed Ambassador Mr. Myron Taylor and spontaneously repeated by him in 1942 that "America has no hatred of the Italian people" gives Us confidence that they will be treated with consideration and understanding; and if they have had to mourn the untimely death of dear ones, they will yet in their present circumstances be spared as far as possible further pain and devastation, and their many treasured shrines of Religion and Art,—precious heritage not of one people but of all human and Christian civilization will be saved from irreparable ruin. This is a hope and prayer very dear to Our paternal heart, and We have thought that its realization could not be more effec-tively ensured than by expressing it very simply to Your Excellency.

With heartfelt prayer We beg God's blessings on Your Excellency and the people of the United States.

From the Vatican,   PIUS PP. XII
May 19, 1943.

XVIII

Reply of President Roosevelt to His Holiness

JUNE 16, 1943

Your Holiness:

The communication of May 19, 1943 from Your Holiness setting forth in eloquent language the deep feelings of emotion with which Your Holiness views the devastating effects of war on Italy strikes a very responsive chord in my heart. No one appreciates more than I the ceaseless efforts of Your Holiness to prevent the outbreak of war in Europe in 1939 and subsequently to limit its contagion. Your Holiness is familiar with the repeated efforts which were made in 1940 by this Government, and by many elements within the United States to deter the Chief of the Italian Government from plunging his country and countrymen into a ruinous war whose outcome, I reminded him even at that time, could only prove disastrous.

The sympathetic response of Your Holiness to the many appeals of the Italian people on behalf of their country is understood and appreciated by me. May I say that Americans are among those who value most the religious shrines and the historical monuments of Italy. However, my countrymen are likewise united in their determination to win the war which has been thrust upon them and for which the present government of Italy must share its full responsibility. My countrymen and I deplore the loss of life on both sides which must result and the destruction of property and resources.

Attacks against Italy are limited, to the extent humanly possible, to military objectives. We have not and will not make warfare on civilians or against non-military objectives. In the event it should be found militarily necessary for Allied planes to operate over Rome our aviators are thoroughly informed as to the location of the Vatican and have been specifically instructed to prevent bombs from falling within the Vatican City. This may be an opportune time to warn Your Holiness that I have no reason to feel assured that Axis planes would not make an opportunity to bomb Vatican City with the purpose of charging Allied planes with the outrages they themselves had committed.

My country has no choice but to prosecute the war with all force against the enemy until every resistance has been overcome. Your Holiness will understand, I am confident, that in this struggle for human liberty no exception can be made to the full prosecution of the war against any legitimate military enemy objective. Any other course would only delay the fulfillment of that desire in which Your Holiness and the governments and peoples of the United Nations—and I believe the people of Italy likewise—are joined—the return of peace on earth.

Believe me, with the assurances of my highest regard,

Yours very sincerely,

FRANKLIN D. ROOSEVELT

XIX

Message from President Roosevelt to His Holiness

[TELEGRAM] JULY 10, 1943

His Holiness Pope Pius XII
Vatican City

Your Holiness:

By the time this message reaches Your Holiness a landing force by American and British troops will have taken place on Italian soil. The soldiers of the United Nations have come to rid Italy of Fascism and of its unhappy symbols and to drive out the Nazi oppressors who are infesting her.

There is no need for me to reaffirm that respect for religious beliefs and for the free exercise of religious worship is fundamental to our ideas. Churches and religious institutions will, to the extent that it is within our power, be spared the devastations of war during the struggle ahead. Throughout the period of operations the neutral status of the Vatican City as well as of the Papal domains throughout Italy will be respected.

I look forward as does Your Holiness to that bright day when the Peace of God returns to the world. We are convinced that this will occur only when the forces of evil which now hold vast areas of Europe and Asia enslaved have been utterly destroyed. On that day we will joyfully turn our energies from the grim duties of war to the fruitful tasks of reconstruction. In common with all other nations and forces imbued with the spirit of good will toward men and with the help of Almighty God we will turn our hearts and our minds to the exacting task of building a just and enduring peace on earth.

FRANKLIN D. ROOSEVELT

XX

Reply of His Holiness to President Roosevelt

Your Excellency:

Our Secretary of State acknowledged at once by telegram the receipt of Your Excellency's message of the tenth instant and he expressed Our grateful appreciation of the assurances given that "the neutral status of the Vatican City as well as of the Papal domains throughout Italy will be respected" during the military operations ahead.

The neutrality of the Holy See strikes its roots deep in the very nature of Our Apostolic Ministry, which places Us above any armed conflict between nations. Yet it is this same God-given mission to safeguard and defend the eternal, spiritual interests of all men redeemed by Christ that makes Us the more sensible of human pain and sorrow. The war continues to multiply these sufferings a hundred-fold for so many millions of peace-loving, innocent men and women that Our paternal heart can find no rest except in constant, increasing efforts to dry the tears of aging mothers, of widows and orphaned children, and to hold back by every means at Our disposal the mounting flood that threatens to bury completely beneath its raging waters once fair lands of Europe and Asia.

Moved by this strong, insistent love for humankind We cannot but take this occasion of the message which Your Excellency has kindly addressed to Us to repeat an appeal made by Us more than once in these past few years. It is a prayer that everywhere, as far as humanly possible, the civil populations be spared the horrors of war; that the homes of God's poor be not laid in ashes; that the little ones and youth, a nation's hope, be preserved from all harm—how Our heart bleeds when We hear of helpless children made victims of cruel war—; that churches dedicated to the worship of God and monuments that enshrine the memory and masterpieces of human genius be preserved from destruction.

We repeat this appeal unwilling to yield to any thought of its hopelessness, although almost daily We must continue to deplore the evils against which We pray. And now even in Rome, parent of western civilization and for well nigh two thousand years centre of the Catholic world, to which millions, one may risk the assertion, hundreds of millions of men through-out the world have recently been turning their anxious gaze. We have had to witness the harrowing scene of death leaping from the skies and stalking pitilessly through unsuspecting homes striking down women and children; and in person We have visited and with sorrow contemplated the gaping ruins of that ancient and priceless Papal basilica of St. Lawrence, one of the most treasured and loved sanctuaries of Romans, espe-cially close to the heart of all Supreme Pontiffs, and visited with devotion by pilgrims from all countries of the world. God knows how much We have suffered from the first days of the war for the lot of all those cities that have been exposed to aerial bombardments, especially for those that have been bombed not for a day, but for weeks and months without respite. But since divine Providence has placed Us head over the Catholic Church and Bishop of this city so rich in sacred shrines and hallowed, immortal memories, We feel it Our duty to voice a particular prayer and hope that all may recognize that a city, whose every district, in some districts every street has its irre-placeable monuments of faith or art and Christian culture, cannot be attacked without inflicting an incomparable loss on the patrimony of Religion and Civilization.

Meanwhile the war proceeds at a quickened pace; and as the peoples of the world are being told to prepare themselves for increasingly destructive battles that will drain the life-blood of many thousands of the armed forces and, to our grief be it said, of civilians, Our own soul makes ready for a more grievous ordeal of sorrow and anxiety. But it is with no diminished hope and confidence that in this very hour We call on God, Our sole stay and comfort, to hasten the dawn of that day when His peace will erect the glorious temple builded of living stones, the nations of the earth, wherein all members of the vast human family will find tranquillity, security in justice, and freedom and inspiration to worship their Creator and to love their fellow-men. It is the day, as Your Excellency says, longed for by all men of good will. But not all realize that that temple will stand and endure only if set on the foundation of Christian, more than mere human charity, not alloyed with vindictive passion or any elements of hate. Such charity the divine Redeemer of mankind proclaimed as His commandment, illustrated by His example and sealed with His blood. Through it men can once again be united as loved and loving children of their divine Father in heaven. We avail Ourselves of this occasion to renew Our good wishes, while we pray God to protect Your Person and the people of the United States.

PIUS PP. XII

From the Vatican,
July 19, 1943.

XXI

Letter from His Holiness to President Roosevelt

AUGUST 30, 1943

Your Excellency:

Recent events have naturally focused the world's attention for the moment on Italy, and much has been said and written on what policy she would or should now follow for her own best interests. Too many, We fear, take for granted that she is entirely free to follow the policy of her choice; and We have wished to express to Your Excellency Our conviction that this is far from true. Of her desire for peace and to be done with the war, there can be no doubt; but in the presence of formidable forces opposing the actuation or even the official declaration of that desire she finds herself shackled and quite without the necessary means of defending herself.

If under such circumstances Italy is to be forced still to bear devastating blows against which she is practically defenceless, We hope and pray that the military leaders will find it possible to spare innocent civil populations and in particular churches and religious institutions the ravages of war. Already, We must recount with deep sorrow and regret, these figure very prominently among the ruins of Italy's most populous and important cities. But the message of assurance addressed to Us by Your Excellency sustains Our hope, even in the face of bitter experience, that God's temples and the homes erected by Christian charity for the poor and sick and abandoned members of Christ's flock may survive the terrible onslaught. May God in His merciful pity and love hearken to the universal cry of His children and let them hear once more the voice of Christ say: Peace!

We are happy of this occasion to renew the expression of Our sincere good wishes to Your Excellency.

PIUS PP. XII

From the Vatican,
August 30, 1943

Toward "True and Enduring Peace"

EXPLANATORY NOTE

For nearly two years after September, 1942, a further visit to Rome had been prevented by the opposition of Mussolini. When the Allied forces freed Rome, President Roosevelt desired me to renew discussions with the Pope at once. In answer to the President's telegram of inquiry and greeting, the Pope immediately extended His welcome (Messages Nos. XXII and XXIII). I was received June 21, 1944, in the first of many audiences during a visit lasting until victory was won in Europe.

Exchanges of views were desired on several major subjects, of which the necessity of continuing hostilities until Germany surrendered unconditionally was the first. The American view was explained as precluding the negotiation of any armistice with Germany. Absolute defeat of German forces on German soil was vital not only for victory but for a lasting change of heart on the part of the German people with regard to militarism and aggressive expansion. In contrast to Italy, in which a functioning government freely repudiating Fascism had existed at the time of surrender, no government would exist in Germany of a character warranting recognition by the United Nations for the purpose of discussing conditions of armistice. There would be no negotiation of surrender terms.

Any reports questioning whether the American people had been entertaining any other views on this matter lacked substance in fact. Any approaches on the part of the Nazi rulers of Germany toward seeking settlement of the war short of unconditional surrender would equally lack foundation in realistic facts and would have no bearing. Individuals guilty of war crimes would be held accountable. However, the objectives of the United States after victory envisaged progressive advancement of the German people to self-government and a peaceful and satisfying life. The nations which were to have the responsibilities conferred by the surrender were obligated to discharge them together.

His Holiness, while maintaining the neutrality and impartiality constantly followed by the Holy See regarding civil antagonisms between states, appreciated the consideration that had been given to the long range aspects of these matters. He expressed great pleasure that no vindictive motives were present in the views of the United States. Although individual leaders were accountable to just punishment for wrongful actions, His paternal affection extended to all peoples, and the welfare of the German people must be protected and assured, as must also be the welfare of other peoples, in the interest of moral and peaceful relations permanently among men and peoples everywhere. He believed that the solution of all post-war problems must be considered particularly in the light of the principle of the unity of mankind and of the family of peoples. Accordingly, apart from any controversial questions involved, He was pleased that the United States contemplated that Germany, as other enemy states, after demonstrating the intention to be peace-loving, might be associated with the community of nations in maintaining peace and security.

Discussion of organized international cooperation to keep peace in the future was the second subject, and necessarily was in the broadest terms until the views of the major powers had been clarified in the Dumbarton Oaks Proposals. The President and Secretary Hull had already suggested, however, many essential features of a desirable international organization to maintain peace and security and to promote the conditions of stability and of well-being necessary for peaceful and friendly relations. The President hoped that creation of such an international organization during the war, by guaranteeing security in the future for all nations, would solve or help to solve many problems left by the war, and aid in hastening reconstruction.

The Pope expressed His desire to encourage any project which gave firm promise of the furtherance of a just and enduring peace by being founded on international agreement and on the moral law. American views as so far developed concorded with His own in basic respects, including the necessity that peace be supported by armed power. He emphasized, as in His subsequent Christmas address, that peace required a return to belief in the solidarity of all peoples. It also required full recognition of the equal right of sovereignty among member states, mutual guarantees, and assurance of justice whenever sanction had to be employed.

While these discussions were proceeding, His Holiness was making all possible effort to succor the refugees who had survived the period of Nazi control in Italy or who could be assisted in other lands. The President referred specially to this in his message of August 3, 1944 (Message No. XXIV). The reply of the Pope (Message No. XXV) reflected the comfort He found in the President's realization of the difficulties and hardships which beset all peoples in or near the scenes of combat and of His resulting concerns and problems.

These concerns and problems related, aside from those above, to religious freedom, to stability and order after hostilities, and to relief.

Delay in the coming of the time when full and unrestricted right to worship God as conscience dictated would be respected in all countries continued to urge His Holiness to explore every possibilitity of constructive steps to that end. He especially felt that, following the social and economic distress, the breakdown of human standards, and the disorganization consequent from prolonged war, doctrines of communistic character might impede the respect for freedom of religion, a human right fundamental to a peaceful and enduring world order. When in due course the purposes embodied in the Charter of the United Nations included the promotion of respect for human rights and for fundamental freedoms for all without distinction as to religion, progress toward this great goal was substantially advanced.

Seeking to encourage the taking of measures of foresight toward assuring stability and order in the many countries confronting serious dislocation after their ordeal of war, He hoped that the United States would participate with other United Nations so long as necessary in assisting Italy and the other countries until stable governments expressing the will of the people could be constituted. In response, assurance was extended on the President's behalf that the United States intended to give appropriate assistance to that end.

The relief needs of the millions of displaced peoples, prisoners of war, men and women engaged in forced labor away from their home lands, and civilian internees in all parts of Europe were matters of deep feeling to His Holiness, and of tireless activity. To these were added the great temporary needs of liberated peoples for medicines and foods and other essential supplies to maintain health. In Italy this problem had been increasing steadily beyond the probable capabilities of UNRRA, then still organizing and unable to help for many months. Almost all of the need had to be met otherwise. Consequently, American Relief for Italy was organized in April, 1944, at the President's request, to send materials and supplies voluntarily given by the American people for distribution free to those in need.

To distribute these supplies, the resources of the Italian Government, the Italian Red Cross and organized Labor, with the active cooperation of the Vatican at all times, were temporarily combined in a National Agency for the Distribution of Relief in Italy. This collaboration proved so effective that it became the basis subsequently for permanent welfare organization in Italy. President Roosevelt could announce in this same autumn, when speaking of American relief assistance as an influential factor in enabling the Italian people to throw their full resources into the war against Germany and Japan, that the Italian people were already making significant contributions toward the defeat of the enemy and the attainment of the aims of the United Nations.

During these autumn months of 1944, the advance of the United Nations on the long hard road to victory proceeded step by step. In August, Paris and Marseilles were freed and in September, Brussels and Luxembourg. At the same time Finland and Rumania accepted armistices, followed shortly by Bulgaria. On September 14, Allied forces crossed into German territory. In the Pacific the liberation of the Philippine Islands was begun.

At home, in an electoral campaign marked by non-partisanship concerning the crucial problems of America's world relations, Franklin D. Roosevelt was re-elected for a fourth term. A message of best wishes and prayer for Divine help to him was at once sent by His Holiness (Message No. XXVI). The response of the President (Message No. XXVII) expressed his dedication to the responsibility which the American people had continued to entrust to him toward bringing about a better world.

These were the last messages exchanged between His Holiness and President Roosevelt.—M.C.T.

XXII

Message from the President to His Holiness

[TELEGRAM] JUNE 14, 1944

His Holiness Pope Pius XII
Vatican City

As the onmarch of freedom flung open the gates of Rome, one of my first thoughts was to send back to Your Holiness my trusted representative, Mr. Myron Taylor. I am sure that Your Holiness will welcome him as in the past, knowing that he brings with him not only my personal greetings but also the prayers of the people of the United States for a swift end to this tragic conflict and their resolve to help build a friendly world in which men may live in peace and righteousness.

FRANKLIN D. ROOSEVELT

XXIII

Message from His Holiness to President Roosevelt

[TELEGRAM] JUNE 19, 1944

Your Excellency:

We shall very happily welcome once again your esteemed representative, His Excellency Mr. Myron Taylor, and from this moment We thank Your Excellency for your kind greetings which We are glad to reciprocate. With Our heart profoundly distressed by this appalling tragedy which covers the world with blood and ruin We raise Our fervent prayers to Almighty God beseeching him to hasten the hour of true and durable peace, which will unite all men as brothers in justice and charity.

PIUS PP. XII

XXIV

Message for His Holiness Conveyed In Instruction from President Roosevelt to Mr. Taylor

AUGUST 3, 1944

Dear Myron:

Please be good enough to convey to His Holiness my warm personal regards and the assurance of my desire to cooperate with Him as fully as possible in all matters of mutual concern and interest. I should like you to take the occasion to express to His Holiness my deeply-felt appreciation of the frequent action which the Holy See has taken on its own initiative in its generous and merciful efforts to render assistance to the victims of racial and religious persecutions.

FRANKLIN D. ROOSEVELT

XXV

Reply of His Holiness to President Roosevelt through Mr. Taylor

AUGUST 7, 1944

Your Excellency:

We are deeply appreciative of your cordial comforting message. We pray that soon in God's providence peace with justice will come to our heart-broken world, that Christian civilization will be preserved as the basis and incentive of world-order, and that love of God and neighbor will be the governing principles both of nations and of men. We are asking Mr. Taylor who is always most considerate to tell you of some of Our concerns and problems. With heartfelt prayer We beg God's blessings on Your Excellency and the people of the United States.

PIUS PP. XII

XXVI

Message from His Holiness to President Roosevelt

[TELEGRAM] NOVEMBER 9, 1944

His Excellency Franklin D. Roosevelt
President of the United States of America
Washington, D. C.

We extend to Your Excellency Our heartfelt congratulations on your re-election as President of the United States, assuring you of Our best wishes for your well-being and success and of Our earnest prayer that Almighty God may aid you in the discharge of your high responsibilities.

PIUS PP. XII

XXVII

Message from President Roosevelt to His Holiness

[TELEGRAM] NOVEMBER 17, 1944

His Holiness Pope Pius XII
Vatican City

I deeply appreciate the good wishes of Your Holiness for the successful prosecution of the grave tasks entrusted to me by the American people who are resolved with God's help to do all they can to bring about a better world for all.

FRANKLIN DELANO ROOSEVELT

The Death of the President

EXPLANATORY NOTE

*As the tremendous decisions required in concluding the war and in deter-
mining the basic lines of action as to post-war transition and the international organization to maintain peace and security pressed upon the
President's attention, his health progressively weakened. While the
victory for which he had striven so mightily approached nearer week by
week, it was painfully apparent that the awful strain was exacting an
intolerable personal toll from him. Yet, not sparing himself, despite
medical warning, he carried through the extraordinary burdens of the
conference in the Crimea during February, 1945, with Prime Minister
Winston Churchill and Premier Josef Stalin, and met the increasing
demands upon his strength in the weeks at home afterward.*

*The President had all but finished the "grim duties of war" by the
beginning of April. German forces would surrender unconditionally
in Europe within a month. Complete victory would be won in the
Pacific within four months. The duties of war settlement and reconstruction by specific understandings and agreed cooperative action among
the victor powers, and of the founding of the world's peace by the United
Nations that had fought for the common victory, were the unfinished
tasks. The first conference of all the United Nations, large and small,
to prepare the Charter of the new international organization to maintain their, and the world's, peace and security was about to convene in
San Francisco.*

*The decisive years of the war were ending; those of the peace were
beginning. Here death came, on the afternoon of April 12, 1945.*

*The innumerable millions of men and women in his own and in
other lands, who had responded to his magnificent leadership in the defense of the values and ideals of democracy and the way of peaceful life,
felt in a personal sense the loss of a friend. It was with the deepest sorrow that His Holiness received the news. The following day, voicing
His poignant grief over the passing of a beloved friend, He sent to President Harry S. Truman and to Mrs. Eleanor Roosevelt the messages
which conclude this correspondence.*—M.C.T.

XXVIII

Message from His Holiness to President Harry S. Truman

[TELEGRAM] APRIL 13, 1945

His Excellency Harry S. Truman
President of the United States of America
Washington, D. C.

The unexpected and sorrowful word of the passing of the President brings to Our heart a profound sense of grief born of the high esteem in which We held this renowned Statesman and of the friendly relations which he fostered and maintained with Us and with the Holy See.

To the expression of Our condolences We join the assurance of Our prayers for the entire American people and for their new President to whom We extend Our fervent good wishes that his labors may be efficacious in leading the Nations at war to an early peace that will be just and Christian.

PIUS PP. XII

XXIX

Message from His Holiness to Mrs. Eleanor Roosevelt

[TELEGRAM] APRIL 13, 1945

Mrs. Eleanor Roosevelt
The White House,
Washington, D. C.

In this your hour of greatest sorrow We hasten to convey to
you the expression of Our profound sympathy and condolence
and invoke for you and the members of your bereaved family
the consolation of abounding heavenly comfort.

PIUS PP. XII